M000006319

COPTIC ORTHODOX
PATRIARCHATE

See of St. Mark

WORDS
OF
SPIRITUAL BENEFIT

1 - 50
(Volume One)

BY
H. H. POPE SHENOUDA III

2

Title   : Words of Spiritual Benefit (Volume one).
Author   : H. H. Pope Shenouda Ill.
Translated by: Mrs Basilius (Coptic Orthodox Church-Australia)
Revised by   : Dr. Angeile Botros Samaan
Edition   : 1st edition - July 1989.
Printing   : Dar El Tebaa El Kawmia.
Public Library deposit No : 4516/1989.
Revised   : COEPA 1997

H.H. Pope Shenouda III
117ᵗʰ Pope and Patriarch of Alexandria
and the See of St Mark

CONTENTS

In The Name Of The Father,
The Son And The Holy Spirit.
One God. Amen.

INTRODUCTION

These words are meant to be brief and concentrated to suit those who don't have time to read long essays.

Each word offers you a special spiritual meaning that you can read on its own, independently...

We put these in your hands, not to add to your knowledge but to add to your life...

Here is the first volume of these words, and the second is in the press...

Till we meet soon with more words...

SHENOUDA III

10th July 1989 (3rd Abib)

Commemoration of Pope Kyrillos
The Pillar of Faith

1. CALMNESS

Calmness is one of the beautiful qualities of the spiritual person. It includes calmness of the heart, nerves, thought, senses, behaviour and body. A quiet person's heart never becomes troubled for any reason. He does not lose his calm no matter how the problems are caused. As the prophet David says *"Though an army should encamp against me, my heart shall not fear; though war should rise against me, in this I will be confident"* (Ps. 27:3). It is this type of calmness that comes from faith.

If one loses ones inner peace, everything will look disturbed in ones' eyes, and what is simple will seem complicated. This complication is not from the outside but from the inside. When the heart is calm the nerves will also be calm. In this case one would not lose temper but, instead, quietly solve the problem.

If the mind fails to solve a problem, the nerves interfere to help. The agitated nerves might announce the lack of a solution, and the more the nerves are troubled, the more they get agitated..

A person with a calm heart and nerves would be able to obtain quietness in thought and action. His thoughts will be balanced, void of any disturbances. Therefore, he will act in a quiet and sound way, far from anger or anxiety.

What helps a person to gain inner peace is outer peace, a peaceful environment that. has no agitating effects. For this reason, monks live in the peace of the wilderness, far from noise, people's clamour, and any agitating news or incidents. They would have usually got used to this calmness..

The life of loneliness and isolation generally brings calmness, because all the senses are calm. As our saints say, the senses are the access to thoughts. What you see, hear and touch gives you thoughts. If your senses are at rest from gathering news, you will be relieved from thoughts.

A quiet place helps the senses to be calm, and consequently leads to the calmness of the thoughts, heart and nerves. That is why many people avoid noisy places, seeking peace of mind.

Those who love calmness search for it with all their strength, but others, alas, love clamour and could not live without it. Calmness makes them bored!

2.   HOW TO DEAL WITH PEOPLE

There are many ways which enable you to succeed in dealing with people and winning their hearts. By that, you can lead them, through love, to spirituality, as the Bible says: *"And he that wins souls is wise."* (Prov. 11:30)

1. In your own life, present the ideal that people are longing for.

2. Do not seek what people have, and they will love you. Do not make others feel that you are their rival who wants to take what they possess or what they are trying to obtain.

3. Endure others' weaknesses and win them by your patience, forgiveness and an open-heart. They will surely regret what they have done to you when they sit by themselves.

4. Praise others and make them aware of your appreciation. Make them feel that you know their good deeds and admire them.

5. Respect others and treat everyone politely, not only the elders or those you are obliged to regard, but also the young and those who are younger and lower in grade than you.

6. Work for building people, not destroying them.

7. Do not repeatedly rebuke people, and if you have to do it, try not to hurt or mistrust anyone. Do not pick on them for a word or action and avoid making them feel that you stand out as a critic or an enemy to them.

8. Find excuses for others and try your best to defend them in a rightful way, not through hypocrisy.

9. Be always ready to give and sacrifice and whoever you can't help, offer him a nice word, a smile, or a real compliment. Be up to your duties to all without failing.

10. Treat people with modesty and humility, delicacy and gentleness. Gentleness is one of the fruits of the Holy Spirit as the Apostles say in Gal 5:22, *"But the fruit of the Spirit is love, joy, peace, patience, kindness, goodness, faithfulness, gentleness... "*

11. Understand people and help them to understand you, quietly and with a good spirit. By doing this, you will be able to live with them in mutual understanding, love and peace.

12. Share in people's joys and sorrows, *"Rejoice with those who rejoice and weep with those who weep. "* (Rom. 12:15) Do not miss a chance to comfort people's hearts.

3.   FAITHFULNESS OVER A LITTLE

The Bible says, *"You have been faithful over a few things, I will make you ruler over many things."* (Matt. 25:21)

This means that, as you have been faithful in earthly things, I will set you over the heavenly. You have been faithful in this present world, I will set you over eternity...

This principle could be applied in many fields...

✤ If you are faithful in loving your relative, God will set you over loving the enemy. He will give you the grace which enables you to love your enemy...

✤ If you are faithful in serving God during your leisure time God may grant you the love to consecrate all your life for Him.

✤ If you are faithful in rejecting wilful sins, God will deliver you from unwillful sins...

✤ If you are faithful in keeping your conscious mind from evil thoughts, God will grant you purity of the subconscious mind and God will also grant you purity of dreams...

✤ If you are faithful in childhood, God will grant you faithfulness in your youth, which has more combats.

✤ If you are faithful in not judging others by words, God will enable you not to judge by thoughts, which is more difficult.

✤ Likewise, if you are faithful in controlling yourself from external anger, then God will grant you freedom from internal anger, freedom from rage, envy and thoughts of anger.

✤ If you are faithful in the ordinary spiritualities (the fruits of the Spirit), God may grant you gifts of the Spirit; and without faithfulness in the first, you can never get the second.

God tests you first in the little, and if you prove to be faithful, He will set you over what is more. If you show your failure and faithlessness in the little, God will hardly set you over much...

As the Bible says, *"If you have run with the footmen, and they have wearied you, then how can you contend with the horses?"* (Jer. 12:5)

It is amazing how many think themselves able to carry out big responsibilities while they are unable to cope with what is lesser. They are unable to use the grace they have, and still ask for more, forgetting God's words, *"You have been faithful over a few things, I will make you ruler over many things,"* this is conditional...

4.   JOY... AND JOY

There is a trivial joy for perishable, worldly affairs and pleasures...

Like Solomon's joy with what he toiled under the sun (Eccl. 1:3) and Jonahs joy with the plant more than with the Salvation of Nineveh. The same kind of joy is that of the elder son, when he said to his father, *"You never gave me a young goat that I might make merry with my friends."* (Luke 15:29)

One type of the false joy is the joy of some people over their talents as the disciples were joyful in casting evil spirits, so the Lord said to them, *"Do not rejoice in this, that the spirits are subject to you, but rather rejoice because your names are written in heaven."*(Luke 10:20)

The worst type of joy is being joyful over other's suffering. About this the apostles said, *"Love does not rejoice in iniquity, "* (1 Cor. 13:6) as those who rejoice in people's loss. Solomon says, *"Do not rejoice when your enemy falls."* (Prov. 24:17) This wicked joy is called gloating.

As for the holy joy, it eminates from the fruits of the spirit. (Gal. 5:22)

The disciples rejoiced when they saw the Lord, and the Magi when they saw the star, and the righteous rejoiced over the fruits of their holy toil, *"Those who sow in tears, shall reap in joy."* (Ps. 126:5).

The Bible has explained to us the joy of your salvation and the joy of the shepherds when the angel said to them, *"Behold, I bring you good tidings of great joy... for there is born to you this day in the city of David a saviour....."*. The psalmist says about the joy of salvation, *"Restore to me the joy of your salvation."* (Ps. 51:12). And the father said, *"It was right that we should make merry and be glad, for your brother was dead and is alive again."* (Luke 15:32.)

The joy of the repentance of a sinner is in heaven and earth! When the good shepherd found the lost sheep, *"He lays it on his shoulders rejoicing,"* (Luke 15: 5). He also says, *"..there will be more joy in heaven over one sinner who repents.."* (Luke 15:7). The widow also rejoiced when she found her lost coin and called all her neighbours to rejoice with her.

We also rejoice over all means of grace...

"I rejoiced over your testimonies", "I was glad when they said to me 'Let us go into the house of the Lord.'" (Ps. 122: 1), *"There is a river whose streams shall make glad the city of God."* (Ps. 46:4)

The righteous rejoice over temptations and reproach: (James, Chapter 1*)*.

"My brethren, count it all joy when you fall into various trials" so I rejoice over tribulations.

The greatest joy is that of the kingdom:

"Enter into the joy of your Lord." (Matt. 25:21). This is the real joy, where we rejoice in the Lord, and in His company. Although we have not reached His kingdom yet, we rejoice while waiting in hope. As the Apostle says,
"Rejoice in hope." (Rom. 12:12).

5.   THE PROBLEM OF EXCUSES

Many try to find excuses to cover up some of their sins, in order not to be blamed or to justify their failure in doing good deeds...

It is an ancient fault that goes back to Adam and Eve! Eve's excuse was that the serpent tempted her. She did not have to obey the serpent; so it is an unacceptable excuse.

Exactly like Adam's excuse that the woman gave him the fruit, again he could have refused it!

How true is the saying: the road to hell is full of excuses! Even the servant who hid his talent in the ground gave an excuse worst than his bad deed. He told his master that he was a hard man, reaping where he had not sown!!

Many find an excuse for not praying by saying that they have no time, while they have enough time for various amusements and visits. In fact, they do not have the desire to pray.

Most of those who do not offer the tithes to God say that they do not have enough, while the widow who gave the two mites from her needs did not think of an excuse. The same with the widow of Zarephath in Sidon, who offered her flour and oil to the prophet Elijah during the famine, while she badly needed them.

David, the young boy, had many excuses to avoid fighting Goliath!... He was not a soldier and nobody expected him to volunteer. He was young and even the old feared Goliath who was a giant and hard to defeat... etc, but David's fiery zeal would not allow excuses...

The robber on the right had excuses against belief but he never used them! How would he believe in a God whom he saw crucified and who seemed unable to save himself. The robber heard the people's mockery and challenges echoing in his ears but he would not take it as an excuse not to believe...

Fear was not an excuse for Daniel when he was taken to the lion's den or an excuse for the three youths when taken to the furnace...

The love of the only son could have been used as an excuse for Abraham when God asked him to offer his son, the child of promise, who was born after tens of years!!

The friends of the paralytic had many excuses, if they wanted. But the obstacles did not stop them. They uncovered the roof and let down the bed on which the paralytic was lying...

The one who overcomes hardships and does not use them as an excuse, proves the truth of his inner intentions.

But the weak-willed, or the one with a weak determination reminds us of the saying of the Bible, *"the slothful man says, 'there is a lion in the road' "* (Prov. 26:13)

6.   FASTING AND ITS SPIRITUALITY

Fasting is not just a bodily virtue... It is not just abstaining from food for a period of time then not eating food with animal fat. There is a spiritual element in it...

The first spiritual element is controlling the will. With the same will that regulated food, one can command one's talking by not using unsuitable expressions, as well as controlling thoughts and feelings. Mar Isaac said: "Abstinence of the tongue is better than abstinence of the mouth; and abstinence of the heart is better than both."

The second element in the spiritual fast is repentance:

In the fasting of Nineveh, we notice that the people did not only abstain from eating but, *"everyone turned from his evil way and from the violence that was in his hands."* God looked to the repentance more than the fasting, *"Then God saw their works, that they turned from their evil way, and God relented from the disaster that He had said He would bring upon them, and He did not do it."* (Jon. 3:8- 10).

So fasting has to be accompanied by humility and contrition in front of God as it was clear in the fasting of the people of

Nineveh. They also covered themselves with sackcloth and sat in ashes. It is also clear in Joel, *"Consecrate a fast, call a sacred assembly... Let the bridegroom go out from his chamber, and the bride from her dressing room. Let the priests, who minister to the Lord, weep between the porch and the altar, let them say, spare Your people, 0 Lord... ' "* (Joel 2:15-17).

Fasting does not mean just depriving the body of its food, but there must be a positive side, which is the feeding of the spirit.

Therefore, fasting is connected with prayer as in the Church's prayers and as it happened in all the well known fasts in the Bible such as that of Nehemiah, Ezra, Daniel and the people of Nineveh.

This is evident in the saying, "call a sacred assembly... "

It is a spiritual opportunity to mortify the body in order to elevate the spirit:

Mortifying the body is just a means, but the aim is to elevate the spirit through prayers, meditation, readings and all the means of grace, far from bodily hindrances...

We have to remember here that God rejects the fasting which is not spiritual: as the hypocrites' fasting (Matt. 6:16), and the Pharisee (Luke 18:11-12) and the wrong way of fasting, described by Isaiah. (Is. 58:3-7)

7. THE WHEAT AND THE TARES

Your job is not to pull up the tares, but to grow as wheat. When the wheat harvester comes, He will find the ears of your wheat full, and will gather thirty and sixty and a hundred until His barns are filled with wheat.

The Lord Jesus never wasted His time in resisting faults...

He did not spend the period of His Incarnation on earth struggling with those at fault or with problems of society and church. He took care of building, laying new principles and preparing people to believe in them and spread them everywhere.

It is a waste of energy to be absorbed in gathering up the tares.

The devil is ready to occupy you all the time by various problems and offers you endless mistakes. His main aim is to distract you from building yourself and building the kingdom of heaven, by fighting these mistakes.

By pulling the tares, you may lose your inner peace and probably your peace with people too; as you are going to live in a struggle.

Therefore, you will lose your quietness and serenity and maybe your meekness as well.. These problems may create an atmosphere of endless disturbances and differences that may agitate you and surround you by continual rage.

Likewise, as you lose your gentleness and quietness, you may also lose your cheerfulness. People will see you ever gloomy with no smile. Anger and sorrow might control you and you might accept them as holy anger and grief for God's sake..

This may lead you to cruelty of the heart...

You will always judge those who are wrong, revolting against their mistakes, taking the excuse of pulling up the tares from them. You will be always in clamour and you may raise your voice, rebuke and yell at people and become annoyed with everything...

During all that, you may lose your love to people and lose your gentleness. So, while you are gathering up the tares from others, you will probably pull the wheat that is in you. People will look and see you like the tares, in everything...

Few are those who could pick the tares and, at the same time, keep their wheat. Therefore, it is good that God prevented His children from pulling up the tares for fear of picking the wheat too.

It is well said in the Bible *"Do not resist evil"*...

The best way of gathering up tares is by setting a good example to overcome them. As a wiseman said, "Instead of cursing the darkness, light a candle.

8.   WAYS OF SOLVING PROBLEMS

Everyone is liable to face problems, but the important thing is how to deal with them and reach a solution.

Some try to tackle a problem by violence and confrontation... whether a materialistic violence or violence of action and words.

A person talks angrily to whoever caused the problem, using force and loud voice. Clashing with people might result in losing their friendship and love...

Another person may solve a problem by using his authority, giving orders and prohibitions. That happens between a father and his children, or a husband to his wife, or a boss to his subordinates. It is easy to use authority, it does not cost anything. Authority however has many reactions which could also have the same violence. It could lead to revolting against authority... or at least, if the problem is solved on the surface, it will remain inside the heart, and in the feelings and relationships.

Some tend to escape from a problem, thinking this is the solution...

They do not face the problem but try to defer it or keep away and escape from it. This is no solution... as the problem would return after some time, troubling them and remaining there unsolved.

Others try to solve a problem by ignoring it...

One may try to convince oneself that there is no problem. One thinks that by closing one's eyes, one would not see it and it would not trouble one. The problem will remain there, but one will not talk about it, or think of it, or study it...

For each problem there are several solutions... by proper and quiet thinking and by wisdom, as King Solomon used to solve the problems presented to him or facing him.

A problem could be solved through prayer, by laying it before God and sometimes by fasting and masses, as the saints used to do...

Although some problems need a fast decision, yet others could be solved through patience and endurance...

It is not appropriate to solve a problem by creating another problem.

It is not proper either to solve a problem by doing something wrong and through non-spiritual means, like those who tackle their problems with lies or in a cunning and round about way, or by worldly tricks and deceiving people!!

9. WORDS OF CONSOLATION IN TIMES OF DISTRESS

David, the prophet, said to God, *"Remember the word to Your servant, upon which You have caused me to hope. This is my comfort in my affliction."* (Ps. 119:49,50)

You too, in times of distress and hardships, remember the following sayings and you will be comforted:

✤   *"... and Lo, I am with you always, even to the end of the   age."* (Matt. 28:20)

✤   *"No weapon formed against you shall prosper."* (Is. 54:17)

✤   *"It is I, do not be afraid." (John 6:20)*

✤   *"The Lord will fight for you, and you shall hold your peace"* (Ex. 14:14)

✤   *"If it had not been the Lord who was on our side, when men rose up against us, then they would have swallowed us alive,... Blessed be the Lord, who has not given us as prey to their teeth. Our soul has escaped as a bird from the snare of the fowlers, the snare is broken, and we have escaped. Our help is in the name of the Lord, Who made heaven and earth."* (Ps. 124:2,3,6-8)

✣   *"For the sceptre of wickedness shall not rest on the land allotted to the righteous."* (Ps. 125:3)

✣   *"Behold, I am with you and will keep you wherever you go, and will bring you back to this land, for I will not leave you until I have done what I have spoken to you"* (Gen. 28: 15)

✣   *"They will fight against you, but they shall not prevail against you. For I am with you, says the Lord, to deliver you"* (Jer. 1: 19)

✣   *"Do not be afraid, but speak, and do not keep silent; for I am with you, and no one will attack you to hurt you .."* (Acts 18:9-10)

✣   *"In the world you will have tribulation; but be of good cheer, I have overcome the world."* (John 16:33)

✣   *"Many a time they have afflicted me from my youth, yet they have not prevailed against me. The ploughers ploughed on my back; they made their furrows long. The Lord is righteous. He has cut in pieces the cords of the wicked."* (Ps. 129:2-4)

✣   *"You pushed me violently, that I might fall, but the Lord helped me"* (Ps. 118:13)

"Yea, though I walk through the valley of the shadow of death, I will fear no evil, for You are with me." (Ps. 23:4)

✛ *"A thousand may fall at your side, and ten thousand at your right hand; But it shall not come near you. Only with your eyes shall you look, and see the reward of the wicked."* (Ps. 91:7-8)

✛ *"The Lord shall preserve you from all evil; He shall preserve your soul. The Lord shall preserve your going out and your coming in ..."* (Ps. 121:7-8)

✛ *"The Lord is my light and my salvation; whom shall I fear? The Lord is the strength of my life, of whom shall I be afraid? ... Though an army should encamp against me, my heart shall not fear, though war should rise against me, in this I will be confident.* (Ps. 27:1-3)

✛ *" Gird Your sword upon Your thigh ,O Mighty One , with Your glory and Your majesty."* (Ps. 45:3)

✛ *"... the gates of Hades shall not prevail against it..."* (Matt. 16:18)

10. THEORETICAL THINKING AND PRACTICAL LIFE

Theoretical thinking is just a thought without experience or actual study of the fact. This kind of thought imagines that matters proceed very naturally, without obstacles on the way, following certain rules that this thinker put in his mind.

It is exactly like a person who says that the distance between two countries by sea is so many miles. If the ship sailed at a specific speed, it should arrive on such a day, at such an hour... The ship then gets into the actual fact, where it could be hit by waves or wind and fail to move, resist with difficulty or change its direction. It might arrive after days, or it might never arrive!!

The actual fact is full of obstacles and hindrances that nobody knows, except the one who has experienced the practical life in its minute details.

The one who thinks theoretically sits at his desk and writes thoughts, just thoughts... and will be puzzled why they did not work!! He might criticise and blame. He might even go as far in his criticism as to accusation! ... He would, at least, accuse others of negligence, carelessness or lack of knowledge!!

In these theoretical accusations, he would not be aware of the practical obstacles, as the saying goes, "Woe to the thinker who is worse than a fool."

If this person was aware of the nature of the situation and the practical results and obstacles, he might have connected his thoughts together...

One obstacle may change many wise plans...

A practical person who has faced reality and experienced life would perfectly understand that matters do not proceed according to his plans and prefererences?

He knows the ground that he walks on... He assumes some plans, this is also taken into consideration... Any failure he faces will add to his experience and knowledge and make his future thinking more practical...

The theoretician might think that reformation is carried out by issuing a number of orders and decisions... while the practical thinker asks what would be the effectiveness of these decisions...

When he takes a decision, he follows it practically to see its line of progress. Does it move naturally or stop? If it does stop, why? What is the solution? Does it need any modification?

My brother, do not be theoretical in your thinking. Do not be hasty in criticising others, but study the facts and be practical.

11.   HUMAN ANGER

Sometimes, a holy anger happens for God's sake, but it does not have nervousness and loss of temper, it is a holy zeal.

James, the apostle, said about human anger *"...for the wrath of man does not produce the righteousness of God."* (James 1:20)

Our saintly fathers, have many sayings on rebuking anger.

St. Aughoris said, "The prayer of the angry is a defiled and rejected incense and the offering of the angry is unaccepted." He also said: "Anger is an action of the insane... It makes humans like beasts... the eyes of the angry are evil, full of blood, while the face of the gentle is radiant and his eyes look with dignity."

St. Agathon used to say, "Even if the angry raised the dead, it is not accepted by God and nobody will come forward to him."

An elderly man said, "The one whose heart is not saddened when his brother disputes with him is like the angels. If he disputes with him, too, he later and reconciles immediately. This is the action of strugglers. On the other hand, he who upsets his brothers, gets angry with them and hatred settles in his heart, is a follower of the devil, disobedient to God and

God will not forgive his sins as far as he does not forgive the sins of his brothers... "

St. Ephram, the Syrian said, "The wrathful kills himself. He is a stranger to blame and has poor health because his body withers all the time. His spirit is sad and is hated by all."

St. Ephram also said, "he who hides envy in his heart is like the one who keeps a serpent in his lap. Smoke drives the bees away and hatred drives knowledge away from the heart."

St. Isaiah said, "Anger is desiring to achieve what you want by force, without exercising humility."

St. Augustine said, "What is anger? It is the desire for revenge... If God, despite our offences, does not wish to wreak vengeance on us... do we ask for revenge for ourselves and sin against God everyday?!"

St. Gregory, the Bishop of Nyssa said, "Anger makes the black bitterness spread all over the body."

St. John of Assiut said, "the weapon of anger hurts its possessor... anger in the heart is like a woodworm in timber."

If we refer to the Holy Bible, we will find that it says, *"Do not hasten in your spirit to be angry. For anger rests in the bosom of fools."* (Ecce. 7:9). It also says, *"Make no friendship with an angry man. And with a furious man do not go."* (Prov 22:24).

12. STUBBORNNESS

A humble person may give up his opinion and would possibly admit that he was wrong, and rectify the error...

A meek person deals simply with everyone and never argues much or acts stubbornly.

He considers the other opinion with respect and dignity as an unbiased person, not as an opponent. He honestly searches for what is good in it and if he finds it right, he accepts it...

Some people, when you talk to them, make you feel that their minds are completely locked us to any understanding. Nothing is acceptable to them except their own opinion, and in a stubborn way they reject anything else without any discussion...

A person may continue in his stubbornness, no matter how many are opposing his opinion, no matter what their positions are and whether their talk is convincing or not...

This obstinacy could be due to buried pride, which considers giving up one's opinion against dignity and self respect.

One might continue in one's stubbornness for a long time.,

One might see the bad effects of insisting on and sticking to one's wrong opinion and, in one's stubbornness, would not care.

The heretics are an example of those stubborn people who did not listen to neither the churches nor the synagogues and carelessly split the church.

A stubborn person loses people as well as himself. He could also lose his faith and consequently lose his eternity.

At the same time he loses the purity of his heart... no humility, no love, no understanding and no gentleness.

There is a big difference between stubbornness and firmness in what is right. Stubbornness is the persistence on what is wrong...

It is amazing how stubborn people justify their stubbornness as strength of personality, and they might imagine themselves heroes in their resistance...

Some people, with a weak personality, might admire them. When they see themselves surrounded by many, their stubbornness grows more and more. They might think that many support them, or it is an evidence of the rightness of their opinion and attitude...

The Bible connects stubbornness to hardness of the heart...

The stubborn sinners who insist on their faults, are hard in heart and the work of grace does not soften them... The Apostle says to them, *".. if you will hear his voice, do not harden your hearts..."* (Heb. 3:7)

13. THE CROSS IN OUR LIFE
PART A

On the occasion of the feast of the Cross, we mention the following points:

✢   Our first relationship with the Cross starts by baptism, where our old Adam is crucified so that sin will never enslave us.

✢   The Church has carried the Cross during the martyrdom period and in all the persecutions that followed it during the lapse of time...

✢   The beauty of the Cross is that the Church carried it with joy and patience,... without any complaint or grumbling...

The Cross changed into a longing that the Church desires and proceeds towards.

The way in which the Christians received death puzzled the pagans. It was a reflection of the Christians' faith in eternal joy and disdain of the world, with all its pleasures and enjoyment's...

The prisons turned into temples, where hymns and prayers echoed from the Christians who were joyful to receive death.

✤   The third field where we carry the Cross is the narrow gate...

A person might constrain himself for the sake of God. He isolates himself from the world and all its desires. He disclaims everything for God's sake... by fasting, devoutness, self control and enduring others' offences.

✤   The Cross of weariness could also be included in this field...

One toils in one's services for God and labours (in crucifying the flesh with its passions). The Apostle says *that, "He toils in struggling and crucifying the thought and overcoming oneself," knowing all the time that he "will receive his own reward according to his own labour."* (I Cor. 3:8)

Christianity could never be separated from the Cross...

The Lord Jesus told us plainly that *"... In the world you will have tribulation"* and he also said, *"and you will be hated by all for My name's sake."* (Matt. 10:22)

✤   We welcome and rejoice with the Cross, and see our strength in it. As the Apostle said, *"For the message of the Cross is foolishness to those who are perishing, but to us who are being saved, it is the power of God."* (I Cor. 1: 18)

39

14. EARNESTNESS

Perhaps our relationship with some people could be described as earnest. But would our relationship with God have the same seriousness?

Are our promises to God earnest? Are our personal decisions about our spiritual life serious decisions? Or do we promise and never keep our promise; decide and never take action, as if we are not committed to anything?

Are our vows to God firm and serious? Or do we take important pledges with God at critical moments of our life and when the crisis is over, we cancel these pledges or try to change them?

When we proceed to receive the Holy Communion, with wholehearted intentions to lead a holy life with God, do we keep this feeling or do we forget the undertakings of our hearts and seriously neglect the life of repentance?!...

Do we have a clear cut line that we firmly follow, or are we like a feather that the wind shifts without seriousness?

Is this seriousness, in our spiritual life, bound to certain principles of purity without going astray, no slackness in the means of grace and serving without being slothful?

The saints who repented, like St. Moses the Black, St. Augustine and St. Mary the Egyptian, were serious about their repentance. They never turned back to their old lifestyle, which they deserted with no return...

Those who formed friendship and companionship with God never betrayed this friendship. They seriously remained loyal to Him, feeling an emotional and practical commitment towards His love...

Those who are serious in their spiritual life are never moved by tribulations or temptations. They never forget that they are the temples of God and His Spirit dwells in them. They never forget that they are the children of God and they must keep His image and example...

Those who are serious in their spiritual life show this seriousness in each aspect of their life: in their talk, their behaviour, their service, their worship, their relationship with others and their firm stand towards the thoughts and feelings that fight the heart.

They have principles and they are committed to these principles.

Let us all then live in earnestness... It is one of the qualities of God's children. It is an evidence of steadfastness...

15.   GENTLE WORDS

✠   The spiritual person never uses harsh words, but gentle ones, because gentleness is one of the fruits of the Holy Spirit. Are you known by the gentleness of your words and dealings?

✠   Look at the Lord Jesus when He was talking to the samaritan woman. Although she was very sinful, Jesus said to her, *"You have well said, 'I have no husband', for you have had five husbands and the one whom you now have is not your husband.."* (John 4:17-18) The word "husbands" is very gentle, as they were not husbands but the Lord did not use the other harsh word. His saying, "The one whom you now have is not yours" is the most gentle expression that does not include any word that could hurt her feelings...

✠   Instead of hurting people, try to win them...

✠   St. Paul, the apostle, when he entered Athens, became angry as he found the city full of idols. Still he addressed them gently, "Men of Athens, I perceive that in all things you are very religious... "

✠   When God talked about Job, he praised him by gentle words, saying to the devil, "... that man was blame-less and upright and one who feared God and shunned evil." As a matter of fact, nobody is blameless except God alone...

✢   How gentle was God's talk about Nineveh, the sinful city of the gentiles, whose people did not know their right from left. God said, "And should I not pity Nineveh, that great city." Was Nineveh really great or is it God's gentleness?...

✢   The names God gave to people are another example of His gentleness. He called Simon (Peter) which means rock and called Abram (Abraham) which means the father of multitudes... They are all names that carry praise...

✢   Among the saints who were famous for their gentle words is St. Didymus the Blind, head of the Theological School in the 4th century.

He never aimed at overcoming people but winning them. He never tried to destroy them but convince them.

✢   God condemned harsh words by. saying, *"... whoever says to his brother, 'Raca' shall be in danger of the Council. But whoever says, 'You fool', shall be in danger of hell fire."* (Matt. 5:22)

God does not accept harsh words as He is gentle and loving, His mouth is full of sweetness and his lips drop honey.

16. AMBITION

Man is created in God's image and likeness. God is unlimited. Therefore, although man is limited, he has deep inside him, a longing for the unlimited. For the same reason, man longs for immortality and eternal life. It also explains man's longing for perfection and that is why people have ambitious feelings in them...

An indolent person is not in God's image while the one who has the godly image says, like St. Paul, *"...forgetting those things which are behind and reaching forward to those things which are ahead."* (Phil. 3:13)

This is a spiritual ambition, where everyone seeks spiritual perfection. And according to his perfect idealism, whatever he reaches seems as nothing, so he forgets it and keeps on progressing...

That is how the saints' humility originated and their toil in struggle.

That is also how the spiritual growth originated...

This type of ambition is acceptable and is needed as a virtue and nobody objects to it.

But there is the wrong ambition for material things.

For example, the rich fool who said, *"I will pull down my barns and build greater.. and I will say to my soul you have many goods laid up for many years."* (Luke 12:18)

What are the faults in the materialistic ambition?

[1] The first fault is that the heart becomes attached to material things in a way that controls its feelings and time, and kills any other spiritual desire.

[2] The second fault is that a person gets involved in competitions that would cause him the loss of his love for others and tempts him to build his own personal glory on the rubble of others, clashing with people and destroying them. Like a person whose ambition is to be first or to be head, so he tries to get rid of all his rivals...

[3] The third fault is when ambition turns into greediness or avidity that is never satisfied, no matter how much this person gains or achieves.

[41 The fourth fault is when the means to reach one's ambition is wrong or not spiritual. By this, man destroys some of his ideals and spiritualism to reach his target...

[51 Ambition could be for authority and changes the person into a dictator, destroying whoever stands in his way of influence...

[6] One might forget his eternity in all these types of ambitions and his bearings become completely worldly.

17. YOUR LANGUAGE REVEALS YOU

Your talk shows and reveals your personality. It uncovers what is inside you, *"For by your words, you will be justified, and by your words, you will be condemned!"* (Matt. 12:37)

Talk is not to be taken slightly. By judging you could be judged and by the word 'fool', you might be in danger of hell fire. Some talk says the Lord ,defiles the person. James the apostle describes the tongue as 'fire' that "kindles from hell."

The faults of the tongue are many. They made the saints favour silence:

There is blasphemy, lying, abuse mockery, scornful talk, harsh and angry words, bitterness and envy, talk of pride and boasting, exaggeration, words of hypocrisy and deceit, false witness and repudiating others, foolish disputes and prattle... etc.

There are faults that affect the person himself and faults that are stumbling blocks for others.

For example, the talk a person pours into the ears of others defiles the purity of their hearts and thoughts or spoils their faith and the soundness of their knowledge. It could also damage their relationship with others and cause friction between them. It could also make them change their minds about their friends. Many are the victims of talk!

The Bible advises us to slow down in speaking, at least to get a chance to think... St. James, the Apostle said, *".,.let every man be swift to hear, slow to speak, slow to wrath."* (James 1: 19)

The one who hastens or rushes in his talk, is bound to err. He might regret it, but after being recorded against him, he cannot get it back...

However, there is useful talk. The spirit-borne used to come to our fathers from the farthest ends of the world, asking for a word of benefit...

There are words of the spirit and words of grace, like the words that God puts in the mouth of people to pass on to others, *"It is not you who speak but the Spirit of your Father, "* who spoke through the prophets...

Therefore, the Psalmist says, *"O Lord, open my lips and my mouth shall show forth your praise."* Is it then God who opens your lips?...

Among the gentle words: a word of blessing, a word of comfort, a word of encouragement, a word of solution, a word of guidance, a word of teaching, and also a word of rebuke, if it is said with love.

The word which is from God never returns empty. It is strong, live and effective. It penetrates the heart, bears fruit and changes souls.

Talk then when it is right to talk and know how to talk and when.

18.   THE PRACTICAL PERSON

There are people who live in a fantasy, floating in hopes created by imagination, building castles in the air and living in day dreams.   They never achieve anything because they are not practical.

On the contrary, there are people who are practical, living in reality and acting according to facts...

He who lives in imaginary expectations is not practical.

Likewise:

The one who cries over the past, without working for the present, is not practical. Crying would not help him.

He who collapses when faced with a problem, without thinking of its solution, is not practical. Collapsing is not going to save him...

He who acts without thinking of the outcome or the reaction to what he is doing, is not practical.

He who deals with people according to his own mentality, without taking into consideration their own mentality and way of thinking, is not practical.

The one who believes those who praise him, and makes friends with whoever smiles at him, thinking that as far as he is convinced of something, it must be true (and the others must be convinced of it)... is not practical.

He who thinks that he has to win and be obeyed, just because he is Mr. so and so... is not practical.

The practical person lives in reality with all its surroundings, obstacles and problems, without ignoring anything...

The practical person deals with people as they are, not as they ought to be. He does not expect fanciful idealism in those with whom he deals, but he realises they are human, like everybody else, with all the weaknesses and defects of the human nature.

The practical person does not tackle his problems by weeping and lamentation, clamour and complaint. He faces his problems with composed thought and wisdom as well as practical solutions. He prays that God may bless his work and grant him success.

The practical person does not live on the word (IF)... He does not spend his life in the past, but he learns a lesson from it and works for the present and the future, with all his might...

19. LEARNING

Learning starts during the person's life, but it never ends...

This learning takes different shapes, which vary according to the stages of life that one experiences...

Childhood represents the type of learning that believes in everything...

It is the type of learning that requires education, asks and seeks knowledge, accepts everything without argument and picks up many things by following the example of others.

During the primary and preparatory period, another type of learning takes place, which understands and absorbs. In secondary school, learning is based on discussion and argument, then storing information after examining it...

During the university period, it is another type of learning which partakes in examining and preparing information and, to a certain extent, depends on itself.

After the university years, another type of learning begins, when the person sets out to practical life.

This period does not follow defined programmes or fixed dates for exams. One is practically tested at any time, in anything and without previous preparation or readiness...

You too, need to be prepared for the trials of life...

You might be able to learn from others' experiences, beside learning from the elderly, the instructors and spiritual fathers. You can also learn from books...

Man needs to drink from all springs of knowledge, with wisdom and care, by examining and sifting information.

You need to know life and learn how to act and deal with people and superiors and how to talk to them:

When does a person talk and how; when does one need to be firm and when to be flexible; when to be precise, when to punish and when to forgive...

The one who loves learning learns from everything...

He learns from the ant how to be active, and learns to have faith from the birds who neither sow nor reap nor gather into barns, yet our Heavenly Father feeds them...

Happy is the one who learns throughout his life...

He learns more than what others teach. He increases every day in knowledge and insight. He will acquire the humility by which he accepts learning from anyone and from everything…

✠ ✠ ✠

20. REAL JOY AND FALSE JOY

The real joy is one of the fruits of the Holy Spirit in the heart. The Bible says, *"But the fruit of the Spirit is love, joy, peace... "* (Gal. 5:22)

It is a joy in the Lord, as the Apostle said. But there are many examples of false joy: Jonahs joy with the plant that gave shade for his head and Solomon's joy with all his toil under the sun. He finally realised that all is vanity and grasping for the wind. And he also said, *"The heart of fools is in the house of mirth."* (Eccl. 7:4)

Another example of the false joy is when the elder son said to his father, *"You never gave me a young goat, that I might make merry with my friends."* (Luke 15:29)

There is another type of joy which is considered a sin:

Solomon said, *"Do not rejoice when your enemy falls."* (Prov. 24:17) The Apostle, when talking about joy, said *"Love does not rejoice in iniquity."* (1 Cor. 13:6)

The Lord Jesus rebuked his disciples when they were joyful that the devils were subject to them. He said to them, *"...do not rejoice in this... but rather rejoice because your names are written in heaven."* (Luke 10:20)

The real joy then is the holy joy in the Lord...

It is also the joy of spiritual life with all the means of grace...

The Psalmist says, *"I was glad when they said to me 'Let us go into the house of the Lord'"* (Ps. 122: 1) He also says, *"I rejoice at Your word as one who finds great treasure"* (Ps. 119:162) and also says, *"I will lift up my hands in Your name. My soul shall be satisfied as with marrow and fatness."* (Ps.63:4,5) Therefore, he sees his joy in whatever draws him to God.

Man also rejoices in repentance as it is reconciliation with God...

Heaven also shares in this joy with salvation, *"there will be more joy in Heaven over one sinner who repents than over ninety-nine just persons who need no repentance... "* (Luke 15:7)

Hope is also another source of joy, *"Rejoicing in hope."* (Rom. 12:12)

Nevertheless, tribulations themselves, make the faithful rejoice, *"My brethren, count it all joy when you fall into various trials."* (James 1:2)

The greatest joy is meeting God in His Kingdom, when the Lord says to the faithful, "Enter into the joy of your Lord.

21.   SOME EXERCISES IN SILENCE

It is hard for whoever lives in our society to keep silent completely, but he can exercise silence by adopting the following:

1.   Short concise answers:
If a word or a phrase would suffice for an answer, there is no need to go into extended detail and lengthy explanation; one sentence is enough.

2.   To cease talk on any subject:
There are some subjects which are not your concern, therefore do not speak about them, especially matters relating to the secrets of others. Also abstain from talking on subjects which are not your speciality, such as pure scientific or artistic or political matters that surpass your knowledge.

3.   Keep away from faults of the tongue:
Such as: condemnation, sneering, futile talk, chattering, worthless argument, words of anger and contempt, etc...

4.   Avoid starting a conversation except for necessity:
If somebody talked to you, answer him briefly; and if nobody talked to you, keep silent unless there is something which necessitates your speaking, otherwise you might fall into a certain mistake...

22.   LEVELS OF FAITH

There might be a person *"who is weak in the faith"* (Rom. 14: 1) or, *"of little faith."* (Matt. 14: 31)

Another person needs to *"perfect what is lacking in his faith"*. A third is *"slow of heart to believe,"* like the two disciples of Emmaus. (Luke 24:25)

On the contrary to this, there are levels of faith...

A faithful person,

Another, *"not a novice, "* (I Tim. 3:6)

A third, *"...his faith grows exceedingly, "* (2 Thess, 1:3) or he *"abounds in faith."* (2 Cor. 8:7)

A fourth, *"continues in the faith, grounded and steadfast."* (Col. 1:23)

A fifth, *"steadfast in the faith."* (1 Pet. 5:9)

A sixth, *"rich in faith."* (James 2: 5).

Above all those, a seventh, *"full of faith."* (Acts 6:5)

The Lord said about some, *"great is your faith."* (Matt. 15:28)

There is a strong faith in which *"signs will follow those who believe"* (Mark 16:17) and faith that, *"could remove mountains"* (1 Cor. 13:2), and a greater faith which makes everything possible, *"all things are possible to him who believes."*(Mark 9:23)

Before all this, what is your position in faith? Are you a true believer? Do you have that... *"faith working through love"?* (Gal. 5:6) Do you grow in faith? Or is your faith strong and great? Or do you need prayers so... *"that your faith should not fail"?* (Luke 22:32)

Brethren.. *"examine yourselves as to whether you are in the faith. Prove yourselves?"* (2 Cor. 13:5)

Undoubtedly, the word faith bears deep meanings...

23. PRAYER

Prayer is to open the heart to God, so that the faithful talks to Him, lovingly and openly. It is laying the individual before God.

Prayer is a tie, a relationship between man and God. Therefore, it is not just talk, it is a heart connected to a heart.
Prayer is a feeling of being in the presence of God. It is a partnership with the Holy Spirit and unity with God...

Prayer is the food of the angels and the spirituals by which they are nourished and taste the Lord, *"Oh, taste and see that the Lord is good."* (Ps. 34:8)

Prayer quenches a soul's thirst for God, *"As the deer pants for the water brooks, so pants my soul to you, 0 God"* (Ps. 42: 1), *"I will lift up my hands in Your name. My soul shall be satisfied as with marrow and fatness."* (Ps. 63:5)

Prayer is the submission of life to God to conduct it Himself, *"Your will be done. "*

Prayer is an admission of our lack of strength. and insufficiency of intelligence. Therefore, we resort to a greater power where we find our care...

Prayer is abolishing our independence from God...

It is meeting with God: either we lift ourselves up to Him or He comes down to us...

It is turning oneself to Heaven and to the throne of God...

Prayer is not an obligation or an order. It is not just a commandment or piety and devotion... It is a desire and longing... otherwise, it would be a burden which we, unwillingly practise, just for obedience sake!!

Prayer is not just a request. One might pray without asking for anything... but contemplate on the beauty of God and His life giving qualities... Therefore, a prayer of praise and glorification... is more sublime than that of a request...

Whoever seeks something else besides God alone, will never be able to enjoy prayer as he ought to.

Prayer means dying completely to all the world, an utter forgetfulness to pleasures, where God alone remains in one's thought...

Prayer is the ladder which connects heaven and earth. It is a bridge that we cross to reach the heavenly places where there is no world...

It is a key to Heaven ...

It is a combination of feelings that are expressed in words

Prayer would be without words or utterance

The heart's beat is a prayer ... the eye's tear is a prayer ... the feeling of God's presence is a prayer

In all these shades of meaning, do you really pray?

24. THE WORDS "I HAVE SINNED" BETWEEN REALITY AND FALSITY

Very often the words "I have sinned"., are said from a true and contrite heart, to prove repentance and to receive God's forgiveness...

✛   For example when the prodigal son said to his father, *"...I have sinned against heaven and in your sight, and am no longer worthy to be called your son."* (Luke 15:21). He was forgiven and the fatted calf was killed for him.

✛   Another example is what David said, *"Against You, You only have I sinned, and done this evil in Your sight.* (Ps. 51:4). We repeat the same words in each of the seven daily prayers.

But there are other occasions where the words, "I have sinned".- were said, without proving repentance and were not accepted by God!...

✛   Pharaoh repeated this phrase more than once. It was a policy he adopted, due to fear, so God may take away the punishment. But once the plague was removed, he hardened his heart, as before!!

When the hail struck, Pharaoh called Moses and Aaron and said to them *"I have sinned this time. The Lord is righteous and my people and I are wicked. Entreat the Lord that there may be no more mighty thundering and hail, for it is enough. I will let you go."* (Ex. 9:27,28). But when the plague ceased, he hardened his heart once more.

When the plaque of the Locusts struck, Pharaoh said to them, *"I have sinned against the Lord your God and against you. Now, therefore, please forgive my sin only this once, and entreat the Lord your God that He may take away from me this death only..."* (Ex. 10: 16,17).

Many say "I have sinned", like Pharaoh, then turn back as he did.

✤ Balaam, whose straying was mentioned in the Bible, said to the Angel of the Lord, *"I have sinned,"* (Num. 22.34); then turned and disobeyed...

✤ King Saul said to Samuel, *"I have sinned."* He repeated it twice, not for repentance but because he wanted the prophet to honour him before the people (1 Sam. 15:24-30). Saul perished and God rejected him.

✤ Achan, the son of Carmi, said to Joshua, *"Indeed I have sinned against the Lord God.of Israel.."* (Josh. 7:20). And Achan perished, like Balaam before him and like King Saul after him, despite their saying the phrase "I have sinned."

✛   Shemei, the son of Gera, also said to King David, *"I have sinned"* (2 Sam. 19:20). He might have said it because of fear or flattery. It was not accepted and Shemei perished.

✛   What else is there to say? Judas, the betrayer himself said, "I have sinned."

He said to the chief priest and elders, in despair and after it was too late, *"I have sinned by betraying innocent blood"* (Matt. 27:4). Then he departed and hanged himself, And so Judas perished after saying, "I have sinned."

25. THE NEW YEAR PRAYER

Lord, make it a blessed year...

A pure year to please You...

A year in which Your Spirit prevails...

And joins in working with us...

Hold our hands and guide our thoughts from the beginning of the year till its end...

Let this year be Yours, to please You...

It is a New Year, spotless; let us not tarnish it with our sins or impurities...

Lord, be with us in every work we intend to do this year...

Silent we will be, and you will do everything...

Let us rejoice in all Your deeds, and say with John the Evangelist:

"All things were made through Him, and without Him nothing was made that was made." (John 1:3) Let this year, 0 Lord, be a happy year... put a smile on each face and gladden every heart...

Let Your grace emerge in our trials and help those who are tempted...

Grant us peace and quietness of mind...

Give those who are in need, cure the sick and console the grieved...

We do not ask You, God, only for ourselves...

But we ask for the all, because they are Yours...

You created them to rejoice in You. ..then make them happy with You...

We ask You for the Church, for Your mission, that Your word may reach every heart...

We ask you for our country, for the world's peace that Your Kingdom may come everywhere.

Let it be a fruitful year, full of goodness...

Everyday and every hour has its own work...

Do not allow a futile moment...

Fill our life with activity, work, and production...

Grant us the blessing of a productive and holy toil.

Let the communion of the Holy Spirit be with us in all our deeds...

We thank you, God, for you have kept us till this hour and granted us this year, that we may bless You...

26.   CONFESSION AND REPENTANCE

The sacrament of confession in the church is the sacrament of repentance. And without repentance, confession would not be a confession...

Repentance is an utter conviction from the heart that you have sinned.

Repentance is to judge and convict yourself...

Thus confession, is just an admittance of your own... condemnation...

Then it is not the phrase, "I have sinned." or reciting your sins. The true confession starts in the heart, with one rejecting his own deeds and despising his behaviour.

The one who condemns himself accepts any punishment that befalls him either from God or people, considering that he deserves it ...

To grumble about the punishment proves that there has been no repentance...

Repentance also includes trying your best to remedy the consequences resulting from sin... and restitute any injustice that occurred to others.

Therefore, Zacchaeus, in his repentance, stood and said to the Lord, *"... and if I have taken anything from anyone by false accusation, I restore fourfold."* (Luke 19:8) As for you, restore at least the same amount. Repentance without restoration is not sufficient...

Repentance needs a humble heart. The one who persists in his pride and dignity would not be able to repent.

The one who always defends himself and justifies his deeds and words is not a repentant person. His pride stops him from repentance.

The priest is supposed to say to the confessor, "May God absolve you," when he sees that the person has repented. The absolution is not to be said to the unrepentant.

When one hears the phrase, "may God absolve you", it refers to the sins that this person has repented from...

The confessor who is absolutely sure that he has sinned, and his conscience is harshly rebuking him, could change his behaviour and repent. On the other hand, the one who justifies himself could easily continue in his sins, as he does not feel their weight and they do not internally disturb him.

How could one repent while he is not convinced that he is wrong!! The first step is one's conviction that he has sinned.

Therefore, confession is the second step, not the starting point. There is a big difference between a true confession and another without conviction. ✠✠✠

27.   THE STRENGTH OF PERSONALITY

Strength of personality is not an outward appearance, it springs from the depths of a person , from his heart, mind and will.

One might be considered strong because of his intellectual strength, intelligence and ability to understand, conclude, obtain and gather items of knowledge, beside a good memory that collects and arranges information.

There is no doubt that an intelligent person is a strong one...

He is stronger than the knowledgeable person and the well read. If he acquires these qualities too, his personality increases in strength.

The strength of will and determination are also sources of a strong personality.

Therefore, it is said that he who overcomes himself is better than he who defeats a city. An intelligent person without a strong will, could fail in life because he knows, but he is not able.

Among the causes of a weak personality are: hesitation, doubt, lack of self-control, weakness of will and inability to take a decision.

Fasting and spiritual exercises that one follows, strengthen one's will and one's personality.

A spiritual person is strong; due to his inner victory. He is strong because he conquered sin, the devil, the flesh, materialism and the world. He plunged into spiritual combats, and all of Satan's flaming weapons failed to defeat him...

Other sources of the strength of personality are wisdom and prudence.

Therefore, those who are known for their wisdom are right for leadership and guidance. They are capable of attracting others to them.

Courage is also a quality of the strong personality...

Thus, he whose personality is considered strong, is bold and brave. He does not fear or become troubled when facing counter forces. He is also able to express his opinion, explain his faith and defend his belief.

There is a big difference between bravery and rashness. Rashness is void of wisdom...

Therefore, a personality is considered strong, when it fulfils many conditions of real strength that support each other.

This is said to differentiate between the real strength and the aspects of false strength that depends on authority, physical power, violence, pride or assault of others. ✛✛✛

28. CHRISTIANITY, A RELIGION OF STRENGTH

The gentleness and humility, that christianity calls for, are no indication whatsoever that it is a religion of weakness, but it is a religion of strength. The Bible describes the faithful as, *"sharp arrows of the warrior."* (Ps. 120:4) Describing the church, the Bible says that it is, *"Fair as the moon, clear as the sun, awesome as an army with banners."* (Song 6: 1 0)

This power is what the Holy Spirit gives to the faithful.

Therefore, God said to them, *"But you shall receive power when the Holy Spirit has come upon you, and you shall be witnesses to Me."* (Act 1:8)

The Bible also says, *"And with great power the Apostles gave witness to the resurrection of the Lord Jesus. And great grace was upon them all, "* (Act 4:33) as in *"... the Kingdom of God present with power."* (Mark 9:1)

The summit of power, in christianity is shown in the Apostle's saying, *"I can do all things through Christ who strengthens me.* (Phil. 4:13)

He also says about the strength in serving *"...I also labour, striving according to His working in me mightily."* (Col. 1:29).

It is power, in spite of obstacles, as the Lord said to Paul, *"Do not be afraid, but speak, and do not keep silent; for I am with you and no one will attack you to hurt you."* (Act 18:9, 10)

It is power with authority over all devils...

When the Lord Jesus sent His Disciples, He *"...gave them power and authority over all demons."* (Luke 9:1) We also thank Him in our prayers as He has,. *given us the authority to trample on serpents, scorpions and over all the power of the enemy."* (Luke 10:19)

The Christians are strong because they are an image of God and God is powerful...

The Lord Jesus, despite His gentleness and humility, was powerful. It was said about Him, *"Gird Your sword upon Your thigh, 0 Mighty One."* (Ps. 45:3) He was powerful..... *"for power went out from Him."* (Luke 6:19)

"The Lord is clothed, He has girded Himself with strength." (Ps. 93: 1). *"He has shown strength with His arm."* (Luke 1: 5 1). He showed His power through signs and wonders, "God's arm has made strength. "

Power in christianity has a spiritual nature... It is the power to overcome sin, the world and the devils; the power of endurance, the power of working and serving; the power of personality and how it affects and leads others; the power to defend faith.

This power is far from faults, violence, attacking or defeating others.   ✛✛✛

29. CHRISTIAN BEHAVIOUR

Some think that life with God means just faith or love or spirit without caring much about virtues or behaviour.

But the Bible is concerned with the Christian behaviour, especially about condemnation, as it says, *"There is therefore now no condemnation to those who are in Christ Jesus, who do not walk according to the flesh, but according to the Spirit."* (Rom. 8: 1). Then one's behaviour in the spirit is what protects one from condemnation.

This spiritual behaviour is considered an evidence of being firm in God. The Apostle, expects a very high level by saying, *"He who says he abides in Him ought himself also to walk just as He walked."* (1 John 2:6)

Therefore, we are also expected to act according to the spirit, by taking the behaviour of the Lord Jesus as an example to follow...

The importance of Christian behaviour is shown in God's saying, *"You will know them by their fruits."* (Matt. 7:16)

This behaviour has two sides: positive and negative. Each side has its own danger. Therefore, St. John, the Apostle says, *"But if we walk in the light as He is in the light, we have fellowship with one another, and the blood of Jesus Christ, His Son, cleanses us from all sin.* (1 John 1:7). This shows the positive side.

As for the negative side, the Apostle says, *"If we say that we have fellowship with Him, and walk in darkness, we lie and do not practice the truth."* (1 John 1:6)

Therefore, our Christian behaviour is an evidence of our fellowship with God. It is also an evidence of our fellowship with the Church...

Accordingly, the Church sets apart anyone who does not behave properly, as in St Paul's letter to the Corinthians, *"Put away from yourselves that wicked person."* (1 Cor. 5:13)

St John also says, *"But we command you, brethren, in the name of our Lord Jesus Christ, that you withdraw from every brother who walks a disorderly and not according to the tradition which he received from us. "* (2 Thess. 3:6)

If behaviour is considered of no significance and only faith is important, why then did the Apostle consider it the top of joy, when he said, *"I have no greater joy than to hear that my children walk in truth."* (3 John 4)

We are believers, but we have to, *"... lead a life worthy of the calling with which you were called.."* (Eph. 4: 1). We also have to bear fruit, *"Therefore, every tree which does not bear good fruit is cut down and thrown into the fire... "* (Matt. 3:10)

30.   REMEMBER, O LORD, OUR GATHERINGS, BLESS THEM

Our gatherings are not when we get together, but when we meet with God, or when we meet each other and God is there in the midst, according to his true promise, *"For where two or three are gathered together in My name, I am there in the midst of them."* (Matt. 18:20)

God gathered with Adam and Eve in Paradise, and that was the first Church. Noah gathered with his family in the ark and God was there in the midst. God was also in the midst of the three young men who were in the burning furnace. God gathered with Moses on the mountain and it was a blessed gathering, the face of Moses shone with light as he came near to the real Light.

In the New Testament, God used to gather with his disciples in any place: on the mountain, in a house where he healed the paralytic, or in the wilderness where he blessed the five loaves, or in the fields or in a special meeting at Jacob's well, or in the house of Mary and Martha.

One of the most beautiful pictures presented to us in the Revelation is, *"...in the midst of the seven lampstands, one like the Son of Man."* (Rev. 1: 13). It is the picture of God in the midst of His Church, in the midst of His people and in His right hand, the angels of the Churches. This was preceeded by the Lord's gathering with His Disciples for forty days after the resurrection, *"...being seen by them during forty days and speaking of the things pertaining to the kingdom of God."* (Act 1:3). He invited them to this gathering by saying to Mary Magdeline, *"Go and tell My brethren to go to Galilee, and there they will see Me."* (Matt. 28:10).

Just seeing Him could be an aim in itself.

He said to them before, *"... but I will see you again and your heart will rejoice, and your joy no one will take from you."* (John 16:22)

We gather with God in His house, therefore we rejoice in going to the house of God, as the Psalmist says, *"I was glad when they said to me, 'let us go into the house of the Lord'.* (Ps. 122:1)

God used to gather with people in houses:

One of the first houses that became Churches is the house of St Mark, *"...the house of Mary, the mother of John whose surname was Mark, where many were gathered together praying."* (Acts 12:12). And in the upper room, the Holy Spirit ascended, and our saint, St Mark, learned the ideals of gatherings and taught them to us.

31.   SPIRITUAL FASTING

Lent is one of the oldest and most holy fasts of the year, where we remember the forty days fast of the Lord, to which we add the Passion Week, which is a treasure for the whole year.

It is important to experience this fast as a spiritual period. Therefore, we have to contemplate together the spirituality of the fast and train ourselves to practise it.

Fasting is not just abstaining from food, this is just a means to control the body in order to elevate the spirit.

During fasting, do you completely control your body? Do you take interest in positive actions that help you grow spiritually?

As you deprive your body from food, do you give your spirit its food?...

Therefore fasting has always been connected with prayer, contemplation and other spiritual activities, such as reading, singing hymns, spiritual gatherings, spiritual exercises and judging oneself.

As fasting is accompanied by prayer, it is also accompanied by repentance. Nineveh is such an example, with all the humility it involved. There is also the fasting described by the prophet

Joel (2:12-17). God is pleased with fasting in which sin is abandoned more than mortifying the body. We read about the fasting of the people of Nineveh, *"Then God saw their works, that they turned from their evil way; and God relented from the disaster that he had said he would bring upon them, and he did not do it."* (Jon 3: 10)

Fasting has also to be accompanied by acts of mercy. We act mercifully towards people so that God may have mercy upon us. We experience people's pain when we feel the hunger, so we have pity on those who are hungry and feed them...

One of the best sayings of the Fathers about fasting is, "... if you do not have what to offer these saints then fast and offer them your food." This has been explained by the Prophet Isaiah (Chapter 58).

Fasting is a period of forsaking material matters and whatever relates to them.

Forsaking means having no concern about food, its types, cooking and arrangement, which would make the fast lose its spirituality and become a formality... The prophet Daniel said this beautiful saying during his fast, *"I ate no pleasant food."* (Dan. 10:3)

Forsaking food by abstaining from it and from its cravings is, in general, an evidence of asceticism because of the preoccupation of the heart with whatever is spiritual and beneficial for the eternal life...

32. EXERCISES DURING LENT

To have a powerful effect on your spiritual life during lent , you need to follow certain exercises, which, when you put into a life situation, would help you benefit from your fast:

[1] To exercise giving up a specific sin, from the sins that prevail upon you, and which is repeated in many of your confessions.

[2] To exercise learning some Psalms from the Agbia. You may choose one or two Psalms from each of the seven prayers, especially the Psalms that leave an effect on you.

[3] To exercise learning the Bible readings of the different hours, divide them into parts, analyse them knowing that for each prayer there are three or six parts.

[4] To exercise the mental prayer of what you have learned. You may pray during work, on the road, while with people or at any time.

[5] Use these prayers, Psalms and Bible readings as a sphere for contemplation, to enable yourself to pray them with depth and understanding.

[6] To exercise spiritual readings: either by plentiful reading from the Bible regularly, with understanding and meditation...

or reading the lives of the Saints or some spiritual books, so that you gain a profitable yield of deep readings.

[7] During lent, you may exercise learning the hymns of lent and the Passion Week, and repeating them until you are full of their spirit...

[8] You may exercise a certain level of fasting, under the supervision of your spiritual father.

[9] There are many spiritual exercises in the field of dealing with people... such as gentleness, patience, enduring others' weaknesses, controlling anger, using words of praise and encouragement, serving and helping others, kindness and meekness.

[10] Other exercises in purity of the heart:
Such as modesty, inner peace, love of God, being satisfied without grumbling, quietness with no disturbance, internal joy in the spirit, faith and hope...

33.   TROUBLES OF INTELLIGENCE

Intelligence has many advantages in one's life and the life of others.

But intelligence causes some troubles. How does that happen?

If the intelligent, or very intelligent person expects people to deal with him on the same level of intelligence, which they are not up to, then he will clash with them, troubling them and they will trouble him...

He will expect from them more than what they are capable of.

He will be sad in heart because they acted in such a manner.

This is the first fault; being annoyed with people's behaviour.

How did they fail to understand him?! How did they act as such?!

Why do they cause such harm? Don't they understand?

"Although the matter is obvious!" (to him of course, but not to them)!

He might change from sadness and annoyance to fury and anger!

The treatment might get worse with more rebuke and reprimand...

Therefore, those who work under the management of an intelligent person might have many troubles! In spite of their admiration of his understanding and of many of his deeds, they find him sometimes short-tempered, giving many orders and expecting from them more than what they can cope with! He might get annoyed for no reason, (in their opinion of course)...

The intelligent person, more than anybody else, falls in judging others.

Perhaps without intention his brain thinks fast. He discovers faults quickly maybe spontaneously

An intelligent person might feel lonely... or tend to be lonely...

Maybe because he does not benefit much from people... or because he does not like the way they act... or does not find a match to his friendship!

The philosopher Diogenes is a clear example: he was seen carrying a lamp during the daytime, and when asked the reason, he said, "I am searching for a person!"

Thus an intelligent person could fall in pride too...

Either due to his continual success, or by people's talk about his brilliant deeds, or by feeling superior when compared to others... Generally, the virtue of humility on the part of those who are intelligent - needs a greater effort...

Here, someone might ask this intelligent question: Why doesn't the intelligent person discover these faults, through his intelligence, and avoid them?

The answer is that he might discover his faults, but to avoid them is another point. There is a difference between the intellectual and spiritual, between the mind and the soul.

34. WHAT IS THE MEANING OF MARRIAGE?

Marriage, according to the Christian concept, is that a spiritual person, or a temple of the Holy Spirit, weds another spiritual person, who is also a temple of the Holy Spirit. Both are spiritually joined together through the sacrament of marriage, to become one...

Therefore, both must be of the same faith, the perfect faith, because the Holy Spirit should not join contradictory beliefs together.

That is how marriage succeeds, and the Holy Spirit harmoniously and spiritually works in both.

To join together two who are not repentant, who are far from the Holy Spirit and its works, is not a spiritual action.

For this reason, the Church accepts the confession of the engaged couple, and they receive the Holy Communion before their marriage, so both would start a perfect spiritual life together, in cooperation.

Such a marriage would not be subject to the differences that usually happen when the spiritual life of the married couple is not perfect...

We are trying to set up rules for the personal statute.

Some think of extending the reasons for divorce, when life becomes impossible for the married couple!... Why does it become impossible? Because they do not live in the spirit, according to the understanding of a Christian marriage...

Those people want a non-Christian marriage (non-spiritual) not ruled by the Law of Christ which does not permit divorce, except for a cause...

If the Christian married couple lived a spiritual life, the cause of divorce could be abolished completely from the personal statute. There would be no need for it, as the great love that joins the married couple together would never allow divorce. On the contrary, instead of separation, the relationship between them will deepen day after day...

The most beautiful analogy of the Christian marriage, and the relationship between the married couple, is the relationship between Christ and the Church. As the Apostle said, *"This is a great mystery."* (Eph. 5:32)

Is there a deeper similarity than that? Or a greater love than that? *"Nevertheless, let each one of you in particular so love his own wife as himself."* (Eph. 5:33)

Christian marriage is not just a passing relationship that eventually ends! It is a life-time relationship. The woman to the man is, *"... bone of my bones and flesh of my flesh."* (Gen. 2:23) She is his body and he is her head. Both are one body. For her sake, he leaves his father and mother... What an amazing relationship!   ✤✤✤

35. FEAR

There is a childish fear, such as fear of darkness or of loneliness. This fear might stay with a person in his old age. A person could have fear for no reason. It is weakness of oneself.

Another type of fear is caused by sin...

Adam began to experience fear after he sinned, *"and I was afraid..."* (Gen. 3: 10). And each person who sins could fear that his sin might be discovered, so he fears having a bad reputation or punishment or the bad consequences expected from his sin...

There is another fear which is caused by the lack of self-confidence.

The fear of failure or of the unknown future, or the fear of meeting a superior or facing a specific situation.

This fear is also resultant from lack of faith, lack of faith in God's care and protection. As for the Saints, they never feared, because of their feeling of God's presence with them, protecting them *"... though I walk through the valley of the shadow of death, I will fear no evil; for You are with me."* (Ps. 23:4). *"The Lord is my light and my salvation, whom shall I fear?"* (Ps. 27:1)

Fear could also be due to a psychological complex since childhood:

Such as a son whose father was cruel to him so that fear was rooted in him; by punishment, rebuke or insult, and making him feel wrong in whatever he did. So, he became unconfident in what he did, he feared...

In addition to all this is the fear of God... *"The fear of the Lord is the beginning of wisdom."* (Ps. 111: 10). But man develops until he reaches the love of God, *"There is no fear in love, but perfect love casts out fear."* (1 John 4:18). But the fear of God does not mean being terrified. It is awe and reverence; a holy fear...

The Lord Jesus said, *"Do not fear those who kill the body but cannot kill the soul. But rather fear him who is able to destroy both soul and body in hell."* (Matt. 10:28)

The fear of God leads us to keep the Commandments ...

St. Augustine said, "I sat on the summit of this world, when I felt, deep inside me that I do not desire anything or fear anything...

36.   THE CROSS IN OUR LIFE
PART B

Christianity without a cross would not be Christianity...

The Lord said, *"If anyone desires to come after Me, let him deny himself, take up his cross, and follow Me."* (Matt. 16:24)

He even said more than that, *"And he who does not take his cross and follow after Me is not worthy of Me. He who finds his life will lose it, and he who loses his life for My sake will find it."* (Matt. 10:38,39)

The cross could be from the inside or from the outside...

From the inside, as the Apostle says, *"I have been crucified with Christ;. it is no longer I who live, but Christ lives in me."* (Gal. 2:20)

Therefore, self denial is a cross...

Few are those who succeed in carrying this cross...

As for the outside cross, it is any affliction that the faithful endures for the sake of God, either of his own will or imposed on him.

The Lord Jesus said about this, *"In the world you will have tribulation."* (John 16:33) It was also said, *"Many are the afflictions of the righteous."* (Ps. 34:19). And, *"We must through many tribulations enter the kingdom of God."* (Act 14:22)

But this cross, with all its sorrow and hardships, is a source of our glory and of our joy. As the Apostle says, *"But God forbid that I should glory except in the cross of our Lord Jesus Christ, by whom the world has been crucified to me, and I to the world."* (Gal. 6:14)

The Apostle also says, *"Therefore I take pleasure in infirmities, in reproaches, in needs, in persecution, in distresses, for Christ's sake. For when I am weak. then I am strong."* (2 Cor. 12: 10)

Our teacher James, the Apostle, advises us by saying, *"My brethren, count it all joy when you fall into various trials, knowing that that testing of your faith produces patience.* (James 1:2,3)

The Church loved the Cross that it was taken as its symbol...

The Church used to teach her children how to love suffering for the sake of God, and planted in their minds the saying of the Bible, *"But even if you should suffer for righteousness' sake, you are blessed."* (1 Pet. 3:14)

Christianity even considered suffering a gift from God...

The Bible said, *"For to you it has been granted on behalf of Christ, not only to believe in hHm, but also to suffer for His sake."* (Phil. 1:29)

In suffering and in carrying the Cross, God does not leave His children..

The Psalm says, *"Many are the afflictions of the righteous."* But it is followed by... *"But the Lord delivers him out of them all."* (Ps. 34:19). It also says, *"For the sceptre of wickedness shall not rest on the land allotted to the righteous."* (Ps. 125:3).

37. WHEN DO YOU TALK?

If you talk just for the sake of talking, that is one thing.

If you want to achieve something through your talk, that is a different matter, which makes you talk objectively and effectively.

In this latter case, you need some useful advice:

✤   Talk when there is an ear ready to listen to you. If you find that the person to whom you are talking is not listening to you, stop talking. Do not talk to a person who is exhausted or tired, either physically or psychologically, or who is under pressure...

Do not talk to a person who is busy and has no time to listen to you, or does not have the time to understand and discuss your point of view...

As it has been wisely said, *"A word fitly spoken is like apples of gold in settings of silver."* (Prov. 25:11)

Before you talk to a person, choose the right time, when he is feeling the best, to present your opinion and he will be ready, in heart and mind, to listen and understand you, and accept your talk...

If you want your talk to be effective:

Win your listeners, then you'll win the talk and its outcome.

Many aim at winning the discussion by any means, even by losing the one to whom they are talking... which results in the loss of everything. Logic alone is not enough without the psychological side...

1.   The one who defeats his discussant and proves him wrong, especially in the presence of others, could never gain anything good from this person...

2.   Whoever interrupts who speaks to him, without giving him a chance to talk, and answers back before the speech is finished and acts as an opponent, will never find in the heart of his discussant the ability to respond or be convinced, no matter how logical his opinion may be.

3.   The one who mocks the ideas of another, showing how they are weak, trivial, impractical and illogical, will also achieve no result...

Therefore, respect the opinion of the other speaker, no matter how much you are against him...

Answer him politely and courteously...

Try and reach the heart of the one you speak with, before, you reach his mind. Then surely you will win the heart as well as the mind.   ✣✣✣

38. PEACE OF THE HEART

Peace of the heart is one of the fruits of the Holy Spirit.

When the Holy Spirit dwells in one's heart, it gives peace to this heart, as the Apostle says, *"and the peace of God which surpasses all understanding..."* (Phil. 4:7)

Peace was a gift from the Lord Jesus to the people, as He said, *"Peace I leave with you, my peace I give to you."* (John 14:27)

The one who is full of peace does not get troubled, or worried or disturbed, no matter how much pressure is on him from the outside.

His peace does not depend on the outer circumstances but on his confidence in God's protection and care and his faith in God's promises.

As long as the Lord exists, works and protects, there is no need to fear. For this reason the prophet David said, *"Yea, though I walk through the valley of the shadow of death, I will fear no evil; for You are with me; Your rod and Your staff, they comfort me."* (Ps. 23:4)

His source of peace is his feeling that God is with him.

The Disciples were troubled when they were in the boat and they thought that the Lord was asleep, while the sea was high. They lost their peace. The prevailing factor was the outer circumstances and the feeling that God's work was not there. Therefore, the Lord arose and rebuked the wind and restored their peace to them.

Be firm inside, steadfast in your faith, then nothing from outside will shake you. Be like a house built on the rock, no wind or rain will affect it, as it is firmly built.

A good ship is never harmed by strong waves that hit it. But when does a ship get affected? When there is a hole that lets water inside it... Do you have a hole that would let water leak into yourself and drown it...

St Anthony was an example of peace of the heart. The Apostolic St Athanasius, said about him "Anyone with a bitter soul, and disturbed thought, will have his heart filled with peace when he sees the face of St Anthony."

The one who is full of peace could flow over to others, granting them comfort...

Live then in peace, you will be comforted and live in confidence and calm, in good health, both spiritually and physically...

39. CARRY YOUR CROSS...
BE CRUCIFIED, NOT A CRUCIFIER

If you are crucified, be assured that God will be with you, restoring your right completely, if not in this world, then in Heaven.

If however you are a crucifier of others God will be against you, till He restores others' rights from you, and punish you...

If you crucify others, it means that there is an evil element of attack and violence in you. These are all different aspects of injustice that do not agree with the righteousness expected from you or with the human idealism that laymen need...

But if you are crucified, especially for the sake of truth or faith, be confident that any pain you suffer is counted by God. It has its crown in Heaven and its blessing on earth...

Be sure that heaven is completely on your side: God, the angels, and the saints...

All those who follow what is right, suffer for its sake.

All those who remained firm in faith, paid a price for their faith...

The history of martyrs has many stories of those whose blood was shed for the sake of their faith... our history, in particular, is full of such stories...

Anyone can be violent, but it does not prove idealism. Injustice is easy and within the reach of anyone but there is no religion that agrees with it...

Therefore, keep your idealism and temper and carry your cross. The falsity that frightens you will never remain forever...

The Lord Jesus who tasted the bitterness of pain and endured the cross, is able to help those who suffer and are crucified at any time and in any place...

Look at the picture of Jesus, crucified, and you will be comforted.

Be confident that after Calvary, there are the glories of the Resurrection...

God saw the blood of Naboth the Jezreelite being shed and He did not remain silent. His reaction was strong...

Therefore, *"Wait on the Lord; be of good courage, and He shall strengthen your heart; wait, I say, on the Lord!"* (Ps. 27:14)

If you are crucified, Christ will be by your side... He will see His image in you... Be therefore an image of Christ.

40. YOUR SPIRITUALITY DURING EL-KHAMASIN [PENTECOST]

Truly, El-Khamasin (the 50 days after Easter) are days of joy, no fasting and no prostration, even on wednesdays and fridays...

But we can also be spiritual during joy...

Otherwise, how are you going to be spiritual in paradise, and the Kingdom of Heaven, where there is eternal joy?!...

What you miss of fasting and prostration could be substituted by more prayers, more spiritual readings, more meditation, more hymns and singing psalms, following the Bible's saying, *"Is anyone cheerful? Let him sing psalms..."* (James 5: 13)

You could also be nourished by contemplating on God's love which created salvation... the love of God who wanted to spend forty days with His disciples, after the resurrection, *"...being seen by them during forty days and speaking of things pertaining to the kingdom of God."* (Act 1: 3)

During this period, exercise talking to God and be in His presence, by reading psalms, having personal prayers and thanking God for His amazing salvation... Keep away from anything that could hinder you from being in the divine presence...

Live a life of joy in the Lord. But do not make your joy a physical one, by being extravagant in eating.

Fast breaking does not mean persevering in the desire of food.

Self control is also needed while not fasting...

41. WHAT IS THE MEANING OF ZEAL?

Zeal is kindling the heart and the will, as if with fire, to do what one believes to be good... One might become enthusiastic and taken over by zeal, for something wrong, like St Paul when he said about his past, *"concerning zeal, persecuting the Church."* (Phil. 3:6)

While there is a holy zeal, as the Psalmist talked about, *"Because zeal for your house has eaten me up"* (Ps. 69:9), there is also a sinful zeal as in Gal 5:20. And *"Jealousy as cruel as the grave"* (Songs 8:6). Therefore the Apostle said, *"But it is good to be zealous in a good thing always."* (Gal. 4:18)

There is a zeal that is not good, like what the Apostle talked about to the Romans, *"For I bear them witness that they have a zeal for God, but not according to knowledge."* (Rom.. 10:2)

✧   One might ignorantly become zealous, enthusiastic to fight something without knowledge or investigation, without accuracy, just for what is heard, as Jesus said, *"Yes, the time is coming that whoever kills you will think that he offers God service."* (John 16:2). This zeal is not associated with knowledge, like the zeal of Saul of Tarsus, about which he said, *"... but I obtained, mercy because I did it ignorantly in unbelief."* (1 Tim. 1: 13)

Therefore, do not become zealous hastily, but mix your zeal with knowledge...

Do not believe everything said to you about others' faults or requirements of reform...

Think, study and investigate everything, adhere to the good attributes.

✛   Jealousy could be wrong in its means and way of expression...

For example, Peter's zeal for the Lord, which made him raise his sword and cut off the ear of the slave. John and James who, when one of the Samaritan cities rejected the Lord, said to Him, *"Lord, do you want us to command fire to come down from heaven and consume them?"* (Luke 9:54)

One could be filled with zeal which makes one fall in abusing and defaming or hurting and bashing or rebelling and ruining. Such a person changes into a tool of destruction, ruining whatever stands in his way in a non-spiritual manner.

This is also a kind of jealousy which is not according to knowledge because the person does not know the right spiritual way to express his zeal.

It happened that forty Jewish persons vowed not to eat and drink, till they had killed Paul...

✤   There is a wrong zeal which is mixed with selfishness and bias...

An example of this is Joshua's zeal for the sake of Moses, when he saw two persons prophesying, *"Are you zealous for my sake? Oh, that all the Lord's people were prophets..."* (Num. 11:29)

42. VIOLENCE

Nobody likes violence.

People hate it, flee from it and from those who are violent.

At the same time, they love gentleness, kindness and tenderness.

If an objective is reached through violence, its achievement is temporary. Once the violence goes away, such an attainment disappears.

Therefore, many violent persons continue in this manner all their life. They fear failure if they leave their violence. At the same time, they fear others' revenge and anger...

Violence has been the weapon of dictators in all ages. It is also the weapon of terrorists and the rebellious and the cruel...

They deal with the will of the people, not with their hearts...

They force others to do things, by controlling their will... although their hearts might not be satisfied and their minds not convinced. Therefore, if reformation takes place it will be just on the outside. Real reformation originates from inside the heart...

This also applies to morals...

Violence does not build manners, it is a false appearance.

Violence could result from being subject to a regime or respecting the law, but it never establishes a pure heart that loves goodness...

In this case, by submission to violence, one could change into two persons: an outer person with the appearance of piety while the inner person is a lover of sin. He could change to form the picture that Jesus described, *"For you are like white washed tombs which indeed appear beautiful outwardly, but inside are full of dead men's bones and all uncleanness."* (Matt. 23:27)

God himself said, *"My son, give me your heart."* (Prov. 23:26)

God wants the heart, not the outside appearance.

Therefore, one's goodness is measured by the extent of one's love and conviction of what is good.

If a person loves what is good, he will do it without any pressure of outside violence, without fear and without seeking a reward or praise or payment of any kind...

Jesus came calling for goodness without violence. He never forced people to do what is good, but to love doing it. It becomes a desire that dwells inside their hearts and feelings, without being compelled to do it. The Lord did not want slaves who walk in fear...

How insignificant is the good that is done through violence.

43.   THE SPIRITUAL PATH

A life of repentance is the beginning of the spiritual way. It is a transition from being hostile and resisting God, to following His way.

It is however a long way where one aims at a life of holiness, *"without which no one will see the Lord."* (Heb. 12:14). And the Lord said. *"... you shall be holy for I am holy."* (Lev.11 :44).

There are levels of holiness, where one grows, taking the Lord Himself as an example, to come closer to His image and likeness...

That is how the faithful develop from just a life of holiness, to aiming at perfection, as God expects from them.

God commanded this perfection in us by saying, *"Therefore you shall be perfect, just as your Father in heaven is perfect."* (Matt. 5:48)

St Paul, the apostle, was raised to the third heaven and saw unutterable things. God granted him many gifts and knowledge and chose him to carry His name among the gentiles, and he suffered more than all the other apostles. This same Paul says about the spiritual heights that he reached, *"Not that I have already attained or am already perfected; but I press on, that I may lay hold of... But one thing I do, forgetting those things which are behind and reaching forward to those things which are ahead, I press towards the goal..."* He concludes his advice by saying, *"Therefore let us, as many as are mature, have this in mind..."* (Phil. 3:12-15)

What is this "*ahead*" that Paul was trying to reach?

He says to the Ephesians, *"... you may be able to comprehend with all the saints what is the width and length and depth and height - to know the love of Christ which passes knowledge, that you may be filled with all the fullness of God."* (Eph. 3:18,19)

What an amazing phrase, *" to be filled with all the fullness of God... "*

Perfection in the spiritual path has no limits...

Whenever you pass one stage, you feel that you have not progressed, so you increase in contrition.

You become like one chasing the horizon. Every time you reach the point where you think heaven and earth meet, you find it spreading ahead of you... to no end.

If the matter is as such, let us then proceed forward...

If we haven't yet reached repentance, that is the beginning of the way!... would we say that we are out of God's way?!...

105

44. THE MEANS

Often, the problem for people is the means, not the aims.

Everyone definitely aims at his happiness, and most probably the happiness of others too. But his first problem is the means used to achieve his aims.

Some turn to means that are not spiritual... . Some turn to a human hand to rely upon...

Others turn to the easiest and most handy means, not the most successful, guaranteed and pure means.

Another person takes the advice of those who are close to him without examining or discussing this advice... Or he might follow the steps of others, once more without examining them...

Very often, these means lead to the opposite of what is aimed at...

In spite of that, one might continue in the same way without learning!

One continues, either due to stubbornness or helplessness, or just for being confident in others, depending on time, hoping to achieve something...

The reasonable and wise person is the one who chooses the way and the method...

He chooses the right way that enables him to reach his aim.

He chooses the correct method that has no fault.

He chooses the wise advice, without depending on one opinion.

God gave man two ears, to hear the first opinion with one, and to listen to the opposite opinion with the other. The mind is in between, to weigh each opinion and choose the best...

The wise person changes his means if it proves to be wrong or does not lead to any good...

But the one who continues in a blind alley that has many holes and pits, many defects and dangers, no doubt has a fault either in his heart or in his way of thinking...

Many times one refuses to correct one's way due to pride... He worries about his dignity or his reputation and what people might say if he does change. It is like admitting that this way was wrong!... But many are the saints who changed their way of life without letting pride become an obstacle.

Many did not change, and God interfered to change their way... For example, Lot, Saul of Tarsus, the prophet Jonah, Moses and others.

45. GOD'S HUMILITY IN GLORIFYING HIS CHILDREN

God did not want to be alone, so He created the universe as a gift to other creatures which became existent according to His will. It was through His humility that He created man in glory, *"... in His own image; according to His likeness."* (Gen. 1:26)

God's image was man's first glory...

Sonship to God was another glory given to man...

The Bible says, *"For whom He foreknew, He also predestined to be conformed to the image of His son. Moreover whom He predestined, these He also called whom He called, these He also justified; and whom He justified, these He also glorified"* (Rom. 8:29,30). *"Because the creation itself also will be delivered from the bondage of corruption into the glorious liberty of the children of God."* (Rom. 8:21)

We also read in the Bible about the crown of glory and about the forthcoming glory which shall be revealed in us *"... if indeed we suffer with Him, that we may also be glorified together."* (Rom. 8:17)

The glories are many, waiting for man in eternity, beside the glories that God grants man in this world... *"Because he has set his love upon Me, therefore I will deliver him, I will set him on high, because he has knows my name, He shall call upon Me, and I will answer him; I will be with him in trouble, I will deliver him and honour him."* (Ps. 91:14,15)

God rejoices in giving glory to His children...

But people's glory is something and God's glory alone is something else... It is the glory of His divinity.

This glory of His divinity is not given to others. It is the glory of God in the highest. It is the unlimited and unutterable glory about which we say, *"Thine is the glory and honour and worship..."*

Whatever the glory that man receives, it will never affect the glory of God. You might light millions of candles from a fire without it losing anything...

Blessed is God who glorified His children in various ways: such as the gifts of the Holy Spirit, performing miracles, having power over devils and all the forces of the enemy. God made His children temples of His Holy Spirit, *"... to whom pertain the adoption and the glory..."* (Rom. 9:4)

46. WISDOM

Any virtue void of wisdom, is not a virtue.

For example, love must be with wisdom, otherwise it will turn to pampering or to a harmful affection.

Wisdom must be incorporated into talking and preaching in order to know what to say, when and how...

Wisdom is a virtue to be fulfilled in all servants, not only in the superiors like the bishops, but even in the deacons.   The Apostles said, "... *seek out from among you seven men of good reputation, full of the Holy Spirit and wisdom, whom we may appoint over this business.*" (Act 6:3)

Wisdom gives its possessors a spiritual perception, an enlightened understanding, which leads to selection and distinction.

When St Anthony was asked about the best of virtues he answered, "Discretion..." as virtue without discretion might destroy its possessors.

There is *"wisdom that is from above"* (James 3:17) and as one of the *"spiritual gifts"* (1 Cor. 12), and he who lacks wisdom, let him ask of the Father of Light, from the elders, and the spiritual instructors who are gifted with wisdom and understanding.

A person could acquire wisdom through experience, and benefit from his own and others' mistakes. He could attain such wisdom by the continued useful reading, or associating with the wise, learning their ways of talk and action.

Solomon did not ask God to give him wealth or authority, but, sought wisdom to manage his people. God blessed him and granted him wisdom. One of his best sayings is, *"The wise man's eyes are in his head, but the fool walks in darkness."* (Ecc. 2:14)

Wisdom necessitates meditation and thinking, looking at the matter from all angles, reviewing all its consequences before doing it. Do not act in excitement or rage.

Wisdom needs intelligence and broad-mindedness...

It does not agree with stubbornness, conceit and stiffness of opinion.

47.   YOUR ETERNITY

Most people think only of their lives on earth, all their wishes are concentrated on this earthly life. All their efforts and struggle are for its sake, but as for their eternity, perhaps they never think of it...

Your whole life on earth is not worth a twinkle of an eye, if compared with the endless eternity...

Your life on earth is just the preparation for such an eternity, the immortal life...

Maybe adhering to a worldly honour makes you lose all the respect that the saints receive in the everlasting glory...

Nevertheless, you still adhere to this worldly honour and sacrifice your eternity, as if you do not care!!

Perhaps your adherence to some of the temporary or passing worldly pleasures deprives you of eternal happiness...

Therefore, you have to be convinced of the importance of eternity, put it always in front of your eyes. Everything becomes of small value compared to it.

How good is the saying of the apostle, St Paul, to the Corinthians, *"While we do not look at the things which are seen, but at the things which are not seen. For the things which are seen are temporary but the things which are not seen are eternal."* (2 Cor. 4:18)

Truly, in this view, the main difference between a wise person and an ignorant person is quite clear.

The ignorant is short sighted, his look does not proceed beyond the visible things. The wise person looks far ahead to even after death... and keeps thinking: What will become of me after I take off this body? Where shall I go? What shall I be?

And you, brother, with what are you busy ... ?

Where did you leave your heart? Here or there?...

For where your heart is, there your treasures will be also...

The wise feel they are strangers on earth and do not concentrate their hopes on earth, but *"... he waited for the city which has foundations, whose builder and maker is God."* (Heb. 11: 10)

He who gives importance to his eternity is raised above the earth and all earthly things. Nothing in this world attracts him.

The whole world is behind him and not in front of him...

48.   THREE VIRTUES

Three virtues should be in each moral goodness to make it a real virtue: love, humility and wisdom.

Any valuable quality void of love is not considered a virtue. The same applies to any virtue void of humility and wisdom.

Any action far from love is far from God.

God takes from each virtue the amount of love that is in it. If He finds no love, He casts it away completely.

Any virtue that has no humility, is rejected by God and considered food for self righteousness and vain glory. Pride is most hated by God. The Bible said, *"God resists the proud, but gives grace to the humble."* (1 Pet. 5:5)

Therefore, each virtue should be practised in wisdom, understanding and discretion... Without wisdom and understanding, virtue is not considered a virtue...

For this reason, the saints used to practise the virtues under the supervision of wise, knowledgeable fathers, to teach them how to be discrete and explain to them how a virtue should be...

History tells us about those who acted in virtue without knowledge and how they fell and perished...

Many dealt with fasting without wisdom and were exhausted both physically and spiritually. Many adopted silence without wisdom and fell in many problems and faults. To them, silence was not a virtue.

Others dealt with offering without knowledge. They gave God's money to swindlers, instead of giving it to the needy...

Therefore, St Anthony said that being discrete is one of the greatest virtues, as it controls and considers all of. them...

Pastoral care and service without discretion could complicate matters instead of settling them. Accordingly, our fathers, the apostles made it conditional that deacons must be, *"... full of the Holy Spirit and wisdom..."* (Act 6:3)

Wisdom gives a virtue depth and truthfulness...

And love gives a virtue depth a virtue sentiment and feeling...

As for humility, it hides virtue from the devil's envy, and by this, gives its possessor modesty as well as affection in the hearts of people...

Let us examine ourselves: are what we have deep inside us virtues?

49.   WISE LOVE AND FOOLISH LOVE

There is a wise love whose owner profits from it, even if it causes some pain, but it is useful for his soul and eternity.

There is a foolish love that destroys its owner, even if it shows features of kindness and tenderness...

You might love a person, then you support him in whatever is right or wrong. You might even encourage his wrong doings and he loses his soul and yours too. Your love would be then a wrong love.

Or you might love a person and have pity for his physical tiredness, struggle and asceticism. You end up doing him harm and destroy his soul, mind and future! It is a foolish love...

A mother who loves her child and pampers and spoils him... or loves him when he grows and wishes that he remains by her side, could stop him from consecration, monasticism or priesthood! Her love would be selfish and harmful!!

One who loves his sick relative may hide from him the seriousness of his sickness and never gives him a chance to prepare for his eternity. This is also a non-spiritual and unwise love.

True love is wise and spiritual and aims at the salvation of souls. It is a love that does not sacrifice what is right for the sake of being courteous. It does not share in the faults of others ... It is pure and sincere, like God's love ...

50.   THE SUITABLE TIME

The Bible said, *"To everything there is a season, a time for every purpose under heaven."* (Eccl. 3: 1). The spiritual work must be done at the right time.

When the Lord Incarnated, it was at "the fullness of the time." It was the most suitable time for the fulfilment of the prophecies and the readiness of the world to receive the Word and understand the work of salvation.

That taught us to take the suitable time into consideration. at work, when talking, while silent, in serving, in everything... It is like plants that do not grow except in a specific season, in the suitable weather, with the right temperature and wind.

As for talking, the Bible said, *"There is a time to keep silence and a time to speak."* (Eccl. 3:7). It also said, *"A word fitly spoken is like apples of gold in settings of silver."* (Prov. 25:11). A wise person does not talk at a time when he should be silent and does not remain silent at the time when he should speak.

When you reproach someone, you must choose the suitable time, otherwise, the outcome could be the opposite of what you expect. Seize the suitable time when others are prepared to listen to you, ready to accept your talk.

Do not ask anyone for something when he is busy, tired or annoyed because this is not the suitable time.

If there is a time for everything, "anytime" is suitable especially for repentance.

Do not say: when it is time for repentance, I will repent! When I get a suitable chance, I will repent. The Apostle says, *"Behold, now is the accepted time, behold, now is the day of salvation."* (2 Cor. 6:2)

Nevertheless, there are times that we consider more suitable and more effective, *"Today, if you will hear his voice, do not harden your hearts."* (Heb. 4:7)

Therefore, some take advantage of the opportunity. The saints never let it slip from their hands when grace is working in them...

If they are touched by a word they heard, then it is the suitable time. An example of this is St Anthony whose life changed because of a word or a specific incident, like the death of his father. He took advantage of the situation to the fullest. That made him forsake worldly pleasure...

Thanks be to God.